T0154453

THE *ILLUSTRATED* EDGE

Marsha Pomerantz

• • •

The
Illustrated
Edge

• • •

POEMS

BIBLIOASIS

FIRST EDITION

Library and Archives Canada Cataloguing in Publication

Pomerantz, Marsha
    The illustrated edge / Marsha Pomerantz.

Poems.
ISBN 978-1-926845-18-0

    I. Title.

PS3616.O44I34 2011   811'.6   C2011-900987-0

Cover image: Photo by Marsha Pomerantz

PRINTED AND BOUND IN CANADA

To the memory of Dennis Silk
(London 1928–Jerusalem 1998),
hoeing words in the Punished Land

Contents

I

The *Illustrated* Middle / 13

Acacia / 14

What the Tenor Does with His Hands / 17

Inscriptions for Chinese Paintings / 18

Table of Equivalents / 20

mm/dd\yy / 22

What Birds Mean When They Say That / 24

Cow in a Gallery / 27

Rib Cage / 28

Tri-Town Paving Does a Country Road to the
Strains of Bach's B-Minor Mass / 34

Roy G. Biv Appears to Me between Two Clouds / 35

II

What To Do in a Music Emergency / 39

Postcard (Lake) / 40

Petitpas Prepares for Sleep / 42

Blind Clarissa Field and Her Doll / 46

Gum / 49

Aunt Jessie Eats / 50

Tree / 51

Cire perdue / 53

Winding Sheet / 54

III

Tortoise Shell on a Windowsill / 59

The Fragrance of Lilacs / 60

How to Love / 61

Safari / 62

Postcard (Sky) / 63

Couple for a Wedding Cake / 64

Who and Whom / 65

Venus Paints Her Nails / 66

Slut / 67

IV

Turner I / 71

Turner II / 72

Meditation: Anything Can Come Here / 74

To the Bomber of the Holy City Hardware / 76

Farming in the Jezreel Valley / 77

They Run / 78

Proclamation / 80

Possible Poem: Rivers on Which I Have
Seen Light Dance / 81

To My Translator / 82

Rapture / 83

Corner / 85

The *Illustrated* Edge / 86

I

The *Illustrated* Middle

That mean streak in stroke where the live side
meets dead flesh at the sternum.
Line of last resort for
waves breaking each other between two breakwaters.
Where Mommy's half met Daddy's half of me.
Where my hair must opt to drop
over one ear or the other.
Where the bookmark holds the abandoned
res, in case.
Where I was monkey and things flew over
my head into the hands of others.
Defiant finger with two on either side,
one op posable.
Where you can't decide which way to
dash to dodge a car.
Where doubts redouble and
redoubts resound.
Internal edge,
cae sura,
un centered.
This post-*ovum* pre-*corpus*
state, stanza.
This still thorax with voluble wings.
This .

Acacia

Central Highland, Kenya

<u>1</u>

Yes, says Suleiman, met along the way,
write about all these live things

and the African man telling you
this. There is sound around his

words, on the highland subliming
in the morning, blunt sun glancing off

his glasses, cooking his camouflage
jacket as he tilts along the animal

tracks in his Reebok knockoffs,
too absorbed with a lion-paw print

on buffalo dung to name eddies
of air. I can't write the sound down.

So hear, please, a hooshing
in the grass, a ratcheting on pebbles,

some woo-waw from a branch.
Then know: it's none of these.

<u>2</u>

I open a door and this comes in:
wind, clouds, dizzy grass, oryx

pointing, tickbirds picking.
I want some of it

out, want to pluck things from
their red-ochre ground, leave

the red-ochre dust outside
the door. (You don't know

how many times I've
swept out this life.) Some

ants and birds will not
inhabit the same tree.

That I live here too,
in this life, with its door,

leaves my throat ajar.

$\underline{3}$

Stinging ants live in galls:
apartment nodes bulging

on acacia branches. All
the amenities, though you

would think the thorn tree
is nowhere to nestle. Still, I

take my cue from its spindly
limbs bridging air and air—

as mine do—with their spines
spiny and their leaves tiny,

so as to transpire less.

$\underline{4}$

Suleiman tells us *Don't touch*,
then taps the tree with his stick,

and ants emerge en masse
from pinhole doorways to greet

their guests. *Like Abrahams
from their tents*, I would say, but

that would make us three callers,
awkwardly, angels. It's not eternity

I'm trying to grasp, only the open
doorway, airflow undaunted by

the thorns of an abode or the toxins
of the abider. No annunciation,

transpiring is all. That I live here
too, in this life, with its door,

opens.

What the Tenor Does with His Hands

Sometimes sketches out a winter sun
and covers it with cumulus,

then from the center gently cleaves
a cloudbank, leaving listening women

exposed like an icy harbor, men
straining toward a steamy cove.

Sometimes it is fall in the tenor's hands
and they keen over lost leaves, then round

a rock, a breast, a Cape of Hope, sink
back, bereft, pleading inconsequence,

quickening in their innocence. The stage
inhabits an old anatomy hall where

from this balcony you could see
a scalpel separate throat from sound,

a larynx from its silent string quartet,
eight bones in the privity of a wrist.

Life was stanched, death was then
contained on a table. Now sound

incises me, the piano is implacable,
the weather palpable. I pour.

Inscriptions for Chinese Paintings

<u>1</u>

I, Stick, paint this in the style of my master, Branch, but cannot attain the iridescence of his bark in darkness.

11th day of the 5th moon, which returns and returns, but not to me.

<u>2</u>

This splinter rests among begonia leaves as if it were a flower. Fingers know the wisdom of brushing nothing away.

Inscribed in the 5th moon by a mind without fingers.

<u>3</u>

Here is a filament of spider-spit knitted with dust, smiled upon by light. My friend, turned to ash, was dispersed by a gust. A cinder of his lung lodged in my throat.

12th day of the 5th moon, which sputters through me like a breath, deepening.

<u>4</u>

Leaves green the celery woods of spring: brushes, and their lines lengthening in the breeze.

19th day of a moon as smooth as the rim of a robin's nest from which all have fallen.

<u>5</u>

When I moved the black pine into the picture, its roots remained behind. Now it reaches out to help me across the river. Shall I go?

Inscribed between the 6th and 7th branches, whose shadows calibrate the moon.

6

Ice cleaved this rock last winter. Did it suffer? I inspect its faces, which squint in the sun at the minerals of me.

21st day of a moon that cleaves to the sea.

7

Is the eye less surprised by five deer than by six? Here is where they arced across the road.

Inscribed as time attends with the force of hooves landing.

8

The lake is incessant small peaks, repeats, antique, release, increase, repeats, upbeats, each crease, each pleat replete, sun heat, retreat, blue teats, conceits, drop leaps in deep. Do you think it is also wet?

Inscribed this 23rd day of the 5th moon as I blow on ink to cool it.

9

I prove to you this butterfly, leashing it with one hair from my brush. I hold on, tethered to the page, can go no further in, come no further out.

Defined, this 24th day of the crysalid moon.

Table of Equivalents

2 whites = one yolk. When substituting oil for butter use
$^1/_3$ less, guns for butter $^1/_3$ more. 1 tablespoon baking
powder = $1^1/_2$ teaspoons cream of tartar + 1 teaspoon baking
soda. All things being equal, 40 of yours for our lieutenant,
plus one medium orange, which is 2 tablespoons rind. *The
mind, that Ocean where each kind / Does straight its own
resemblance find.* To thine own self be two. If you love me
I'll love you. One pound rutabaga = two cups mashed.
*IN THE 65TH OCTAVE WE ATTAIN A FREQUENCY OF 427
BILLION HERTZ, WHICH PRODUCES A LUMINOUS ORANGE-
RED.* The cost is an arm and a leg, like apples and oranges.
Choose one from column A, one from column O. I HAVE
SET BEFORE THEE LIFE AND DEATH, THE BLESSING AND
THE CURSE; THEREFORE CHOOSE LIFE. *Then in some
Flow'rs beloved Hut / Each Bee, as Sentinel, is shut / And sleeps
so too: but, if once stirred, / She runs you through, or asks the
Word.* So say 3 immies for 1 aggie, a cat's eye, for keepsies.
Business is the continuation of war by other means, duty-
free. *The greater the* pesu, *the less nutritious the loaf and the
weaker the beer. ONE MORE OCTAVE AND WE ATTAIN
PRECISELY THE RESONANCE OF DNA.* The square root of me

is an imaginary emotion. A chocolate bar is 500 calories.
A lifetime of burning peat for heat costs one lung. The
kidnapper will free the girl if her father takes her place.
I have set before thee meathook and machete; choose the
yolk. *The scribe is required to discover the new* pesu, *knowing
that the original jugful was the product of half a* hekat *of grain.*
*ASTONISHINGLY, IF WE ADD 40 OCTAVES TO THE MOON
TONE, IT ATTAINS THE SANNYASIN COLOUR OF ORANGE IN
THE 70TH OCTAVE OF THE SYNODIC MONTH.* I give you
that the sky begins beneath your feet. May I have a receipt?

mm/dd\yy

Wellfleet, Cape Cod

This day, now, coming into my eyes, is nothing
you can see. Not the shell on a shelf. Not the lanky turkeys
stepping, consummate, across the patio, into the woods.
What, then? Something haphazard that tilts the trees
that skew the path. An every-which-way of
clothespins waiting on the line to clinch
a thing. And what needs clinching?

Air could get away. Is air the day? Is blue emerging
from shapeless gray among clouds taking shape
the day? Is the motion of the mouth in a shout
the day, does the bluejay's screech
keep the day at bay?

Suppose the cardinal skimming an incline of air
from fence to oak, from oak to pine, leaving a smudge of red
behind, is buffing the edge of day. Do lichens grow there, does day
grow on a host in splendid symbiosis, does the day grow on you,
can the day be likened to?

My new watch demarks a moment with a *toc*
that was recently not. We who can tell time,
what should we tell it?

The drop forming on an eave, the incremental weighting
of transparency, the nothing-there that splats, is that
the day? Is the next drop the same day
with a different glisten?

A sudden gust inverts umbrella struts
from a downcast 8:20 to exultant 10:10,
quickening the day. If we take our time now,
will there be any left?

When weather is over and sun resolved in sky,
hours eddy under the clothesline,
shifting a shadow stripe.
Will day stand firm
if I let go?

What Birds Mean When They Say That

Silence glimmers in a pond,
louder in the midst of birds:

surface riffled, fretted,
fluted, deep intact.

They say *taratat* and *brrrp*,
every good, hi-ho, fine does,

willow-willow, dash dot, what
not, and I transcribe like a

moth limping, meticulous,
across a sandy path.

Hey-did, fine does, have you.
Pines reach, oaks lean.

What seems like duck-din
from a house at the edge

resolves into saw-buzz
and a man laughs for reasons

unrelated to the riffled,
fretted, fluted pond,

to him maybe boat-float,
a means of recreation.

What re-creation means
to the pines reaching, pollen

sailing. What meaning means
to the frog in mid-blurt.

What the man means
when he yells *you suck*

at someone; or is it the saw,
off-course, he curses? What

fish mean, sucking
sub-surface light, what

the owl means, in no wise wise,
only feathers, hoot, eyes.

The man tosses boards,
whose clatter does not

mean mortality to trees,
ducks back into the house,

and yells *you fucking cunt*
which is as glimmering a silence

as the pond's to the owl
who hoots because he hoots

and not because he means.
The man lives in a small

brick house, pricey waterfront
property, man of means owns

a patch of sand, can't own
a piece of pond, silence being

public domain. Does the man mean
to have his song transcribed, moth-

walk across an open book, here,
across the muffling air, half an arc

around the lip of pond, so I
can signify? Meaning what?

No wise wise, every good-good,
dash dot-dot, brrrp.

What does the man see, what is
the meaning of his sawing, of his

mouthing, of the clatter of his
planks? Ponds are not the places

they used to be, unsounded by
civilization, though they have

always been part smooth, part
shiver, with neither rhyme nor rhythm

for which falls where—what wind, what flow—
which the birds may know though not,

most likely, mean when they *hey-did,*
need you, no news, brrrp brrrp.

Cow in a Gallery

Thicker slices than you'd ever think,
no pink lights in the meat case.
This is me with precision plastic pins holding
hide and all under utter incandescence,

me here, continuous through all interruptions,
through people crossing through my spine,
my only straight line.
This is my spleen, this is my underwater liver

that, eating slow, I worked so hard to grow.
These are my mutabilities of brown, my surfaces
absorptive in all senses, my anus urging wonder
in ever-new directions.

I'm doing this for you, consumer:
only you can get out of this
something like alive.

Feed me, please,
your possibilities,
and I will fatten you.

Rib	Cage
I can bear to see	only through blinds,
longing between	the louvers,
sleuthing and sluicing	sight. I'm speaking
to you from in here	between darkness and
great light. Not one	of those talking
torsos, but I speak my	freedom, structure with
a way out. Let's say our ribs	form hollows in a sacred
mountain, emotive space in	motionless Mount Emei,
let's say there's something	holy in the squish and
then relinquishment	of guts. Can you let go
of your demand for	proof? The argument
includes interstices,	necessary and sufficient.

These are lines a rake makes,	kissing Kyoto gravel
apart. Parallel scratches	of a cat's claw on
a leg of fine design	to keep us from
taking possession	to heart. A five-
fingered chalk holder	drawing staffs on a
blackboard, supporting	distances that make
harmony happen. A	combine threshing
all the wheats of	the given moment,
a subway grating	beneath which
butts die and	trees sprout with
nowhere to go.	Music? You'll
have to thresh your own.	Bread? Some loaves sing.

I'm all for the un-	attained, the next re-
straint. We need left and	right to keep wrong from
us. Can you feed me through	the bars? Once I was
caged on a Kenya savannah in	an inn with clean sheets and
a buzzer that beckoned when	leopards and lions threatened
gazelles. Authenticity in the	guise of an elephant ignored
us onlookers. We wrenched	renewal anyway from the
outdoors and went home	forgetting the fear: what if
we get loose? Give me that	rack of baby back. I too
can snip ribs. If I got out,	where would I get out *to*?
Pardon me for	noting the
last two ribs	are floating.

Contain, restrain, and release	all stars to fly in firmaments:
Joseph Cornell boxing his	"eterniday," putting Aurora
on a pedestal in sunshades.	Curator says *Way stations*
embody desire around concepts	*releasing the spirit of.* Chicken
wire pokes out from	edges like underwear.
Dovecotes covet love, a	columbarium embraces
the *colombe* and its *après*, the	many languages of lighting
on a branch, enlightenment	seen when it has flown, a
momentary lightening. Curator	has boxed Cornell, cared
for and cleaned him of chance,	but left the front, his face,
open, cannot but leave	the last two letters of his
name, ribwork, to float	inside your chest.

Ring quiet in a straight	*line* said a woman
in my dream. I think	she meant musically
but the eye wants to	see this geometry.
I think she meant:	which *I* and which
she in a dream mean	what? Chance is the world's
freedom, not hers or	mine or yours. She
lighted upon it, momentary	lightening, music threshed
through a regional drawl.	Where does the engine take
us and when do we slip	off? Ambient sound rings
ribs, which ring gurgles	and thumps, then chime
quiet. John Cage	caught that and kept
letting it go: *aCt / In /*	*accoRd / with obstaCles.*

I can bear to see

of your demand for

a leg of fine design

nowhere to go.

fear: what if us

wrenched of guts.

Dovecotes covet love,

I think she meant

ribwork to float the

freedom, not hers or

taking possession.

a way out. Let's say our ribs

sight. I'm speaking

distances that make

to keep us from

Forgetting the

onlookers were

Can you let go?

a line said a woman.

Music? You'll name

last two letters of his

proof? The argument

One of those talking

caught that and kept.

Tri-Town Paving Does a Country Road to the Strains of Bach's B-Minor Mass

Straighter edges than any-
where in air or ear. Steam

rising in a cold May. *Kyrie*
in here turned up all the way.

Windows closed. Asphalt
carrier tilts black grit into

the spreader. Chorus pours
Gloria into the speakers. Hy-

pac follows with two rollers,
big and small, backward and

forward. Stops. Canons too
can reverse. The driver, in

parka, steps down and lifts a
Sunday section from the ditch,

stands on pitch, reading. *Hap-
pen* and *stance* have their har-

mony moment: maybe there is
good news.

In the ensuing
silence birds resume. Fridge

too turns on its motor.

Roy G. Biv Appears to Me between Two Clouds

I'm telling you the conditions so that you can
make this happen too. I was mulling whether

happen and *stance,* which sing to each other, can
also do a duet. The lake, with no opinion, sloshed

against rocks. It helps if the day before you've
had rain-sun-rain-sun, and hail that falls white

then fades to translucent blue. It helps if you've
cleaned the kitchen before walking down to the

lake. I sat on a bench dedicated to the memory
of someone, the only cut wood at this edge of

the forest. It was May, it still is, several hours
later, crisp like fall, but time is where I used to

live. Now I live in color. New leaves are waving
everywhere. Shoots of lake reed march up the

sloping shore. It helps to have recently read
about Darwin. You wonder if they will develop

feet. The clouds, in many layers, were scudding.
Not quickly. About like this. I glanced up over

the lake. I said *Oh my God,* not to anyone because
no one was around. I didn't mean anything by it.

Roy G. Biv was not connected to earth, had no
apparent intention of coming down from there.

Was just a swath, could have been bacon
frying in the sky, with that strip of yellow

fat. Which is why I mention the kitchen. Red
was at the top, violet at the bottom. A thin cloud

wafted over Roy but Roy did not dissipate
until green minutes after blue. I forgot to

ask him about *happen* singing with *stance.* He
might have said pure sound is refracted into

tones and semitones which clamor
orchestrally at angles of coincidence.

Then again, he might not.

II

What To Do in a Music Emergency

When your car rolls into Harmony Lake,
pretend to hum along. Charm a window open;
swivel out. Swim under the rickety stave where
notes dock. Pull yourself up through a gap
in the planks—between, say, *Boy* and *Does*.
See sun plink the water like a toy piano.

I was a child under a chair once,
rising between a man's thighs, propping my
elbows on his knees.
                    Sing. There is no reprise.

Postcard (Lake)

Here looking at the lake, the same damn lake, only a
two-hour drive, the one that goes *blip blip* at the edges
except when a speedboat passes and makes it go *blop blop*
and tall grasses catch the light and turn all young-shoot
green, tacking into the sun's rays the way sailboats tack into
wind to move against it as I watch from my lawn chair on
the sand someone bought and dropped here to make a
beach because kids have to have somewhere to dig to China
from, China where they have Taoism and kids named
Young-shoot Green and you can just *be* without digging a
moat for your sandcastle, can just be one with everything
else, only there's no *else* if there's an *everything*, but even a
big everything, by dint of its articulation, would end
somewhere, have a shoreline going *blip* unless a speedboat
was crossing it, and then a mother and her Dexter come
along down the beach and she just wants to read and Dexter
says *let's make a castle with this pail* and she doesn't answer,
just like the universe, always immersed in some book, and
she finally gets interested and says *we can make a whole
kingdom* and he says *just a castle* and she says *a kingdom, do
you trust me,* and he says *yeah* and she starts a whole housing

development for princes and I'm just wondering what kid
ever trusts his mother to build his sandcastles for him when
a caterpillar drops down on my knee, *vermis ex arbore,* and I
remember I once squashed one out of evil intent or curiosity
and its green guts shot out through its head or maybe the
other end, a whole essence of caterpillar unlike anything its
furry exterior would suggest, the furry illusion of this one
now undulating over my unreal knee like a brown wave on
some denim lake and since the guts were shoot-green I
wonder now if they could have tacked into the deathray of
my shoe descending and lived to see another dappled
day—if another dappled day is the goal—since the Tao
holds, even while letting go, that sailing is a more intelligent
means of movement than rowing, to say nothing of
speedboats, because you can go with the flow or bend with
the flow to go the other way, but I don't know how many
forces of nature you can tack into, such as mothers, in case
the point of being is not to look at the same damn lake, in
case there is anywhere to go while letting or something to be
while being, even circumscribed with *blip*s or *blop*s where
your edges meet else.

Petitpas Prepares for Sleep

1

Petitpas was wee once,
had hardly sidled into his morning
when out from behind his eyes
there came a big surprise.
What was it? A forgetting,
he reminisced, like weather
during a sneeze. Forgot what?

2

Petitpas was all angst
and deciduous. Never again
to be so dispersed by such
surprise. So he put the next
forgetting in his datebook. He
tried and tried to recall

3

what page his date was on.
Straining and shoveling
in a cold stone sandbox
he knew things were ended
alone. But what sarcophagus
could contain his toys?
He pulled faces at
the surpassing sudden,
the impossible unwarranted,
the big brothers clapping
their hands over his eyes

<u>4</u>

until further notice. What should
he *wear* to sleep? Perhaps his
hibiscus print, so cupful and
forthright, so unlike sleep, so
wagered and scalloped, so
fertilely burnished and voluble
what with red and green chatting each other
up. What better thing to wear
to where you've never been, like
the river, twice? Even so,

<u>5</u>

dreams slide off the bank and get
swallowed, winking all the way
like big pieces of water playing it sleek.

<u>6</u>

To put sleep in its place
he could cool it in the fridge
like a withered slaw, growing
mold with a margin of ice.
What if sleep absorbed
the smell of peppers, unbeknownst,
red and green, and puzzled itself
with flavors?

<u>7</u>

So much the wiser.
But must he, too, wilt
in cold, unsavory isolation
where the light goes out?
To say nothing of sneeze.
Could Petitpas prepare

for going on the blink,
when there's hardly a twitch

8

to tell you? But halfway
to the end of his pages—
or had he been, and hurried halfway back?—
he conjured up Tuesday out of
pure exhaustion. Tried to
not look Tuesday in the eye
when he was inside her, all

9

twinkle. His watch
tiptoed off, double-time.
He, single, splayed to grasp
that the rhythm
was graduating from him.
How children grow.

10

Tuesday didn't mind the lie,
which saved more time than
frozen foods. Could she warp and woof
in his hibiscus print, or open
the fridge for a beer and find his
forgetting? He wondered, in a doze,
embracing astonishment
and Tuesday, untoward.

11

She snored. He was left awaiting
what he waited for. What music

12

was the signature tune for sleep?
Petitpas was attentive to portents,
hanging on the next note,
the missing members of the chord.
He was the cello
rocking toward its bow,
and the bowtie on the maestro,
dividing mind from music.
He tried to half-rest but
in the quiet, on his back,
he heard the longstanding shriek
of wall forcing corners apart.
Dust stood on the rug, transfixed,
and the strap of a shoe lilted
toward the light. Was it the
same impossible pitch they all

13

awaited? Maybe green sleep blooming with
magenta regrets for the good old
waiting days. Poppies countenance
no compromise in color. Could Petitpas
paint sleep? Only in hybrids of
oil and water, map his ignorance
and name the streets. Perhaps at
the corner of fingers and laughter
he would meet sleep, like a

14

spot of light at the bottom
of his lemon tea.

Blind Clarissa Field and Her Doll

(An inquest)

1

Does the evidence suggest
Clarissa knew her doll
before she loved it?
Did Clarissa know her doll?
Did she know her doll had no face?
Did Clarissa love her doll?

2

Did the doll have a face
when they both began?
Did Clarissa, not seeing the face,
not even know it needed one and so
pull the threads out?
Did Clarissa so love
the face she couldn't see
that she caressed the threads thinner
and thinner
until they broke?
Perhaps there were button eyes
she sucked and then,
forgetting, bit and broke?

3

Or did Clarissa go blind
because her doll had no face
so there was nothing to see,
and, saying *Good-bye, bland world,*
she put her sight aside until the spring,
then forgot where?

4

Did blind Clarissa stir a soup
and drop the doll in by mistake,
its head only, the pinafore
caught on the pot handle
and all the eye lines
fading among potatoes?

5

Did the doll ever play
in the Field that was Clarissa's name
and pick the flowers
and get slapped around for that
until its face fell off?

6

Or perhaps some third party said
Here is a girl with no sight,
here is a doll that is nothing to see,
and urged an introduction?

7

Yes, there was a dress,
there were ruffles.
Not of the essence.
Not even the dangling feet
with their almost-articulated toes
or any bloomers that might have been
plump to the knees.

8

The face is what
babies keep trying to compose
out of a friendly clock, say, or
the roses and scrolls on wallpaper
that never quite assemble,
even in the eye of old age.

9

After eighty years, flesh tones
minus pink began to equal yellow
all around Clarissa's nose. She was
dead tired of not seeing,
tired of kneading a doll
that got only grimy, never turning into
anything of substance, like bread.

10

Does the evidence suggest
the faceless doll
saw Clarissa's face?
Did the doll love Clarissa?
Did it know Clarissa was blind?
Did the doll know Clarissa?

Gum

Someday-my-mother leans
out of the window to talk
to her friend leaning out
of the window downstairs
and a wad of well-chewed
Chiclets falls out of her mouth
into the hair of the girl down
there and sticks. Such surprise
at tresses met, such giggly guilt
above and hurt below, such

connection: *from your mouth
to God's ear* it is usually said
twixt the cup and the lip it is
usually said *life in coffee spoons*
is another angle. The snipping
a presaging of other suffering,
the loss of hair and teeth. Such
laughter, later: the agèd mind
gumming memory for
a flavor that coheres.

O is the mouth sound,
counting o'clocks,
holding on, getting to
groaning, old and cold.
Let go, Lem.
Not so bad, ending.

Aunt Jessie Eats

The feeling in the fist is bread: cottony,
halved, and crushed around butter.
Snapped in a chair, she's

simple fare:
blank, boiled eyes,
the puréed mind.

When you're dead
you rise like bread.
No one tells you
where to put your
elbows. All of you
is on the table
and angels comb
new space among
your cells, like
yeast. You are
never hungry.

She remembers her mouth
which holds the empty
spaces of eighty years.

The eyes end
and the mind
winds on.
Mind ends and
bones brood
through Tuesday
after Tuesday.
I get slashed
with daylight,
wake up
against a wall.

Her fist finds it, gums grapple,
brow pitches, tongue
plows out the corners.

Crumb-fall in the fat lap,
on the disinfected floor.
Aunt Jessie puts her hand

out for more.

I am clean
and crumbless
and smooth,
bubbled in suds.
Smell of yellow,
checkered floor
and bolted door.
When my lips come
back from the laundry,
make sure they match.

50

Tree

In memoriam Dennis Silk
London, July 10, 1928–Jerusalem, July 3, 1998

Bzzz. Not a bee, not a blistery handful of bees, but a
sawman at a tree. In Somerville, facing me. July three.

Part I: The Uses of a Dead Man

All morning I watched through my window the fleshy maple
felled. That had twitched and shaded in the wind and played

its moving parts across a still, joined earth. The sawman in his
metal pulpit, inching upward against the trunk, making ovals

empty, spot by spot, till even space fell down and bounced
once. Maybe, I thought, he's trimming to make way for sun

weeds need. But no, up up, and branches down and down.
What words are steady enough on their spines to know

the end of *bounced once*? Then *grande bouffe* in the pulp
machine, offstage. More *bzzz*. On the radio Copland's *Fanfare*

for the Common Man boomed brass. Dennis in his last letter
said about a poem, *Yes, do more of that*, but didn't say what

that was. There must be, I thought, some Tree Authority,
some Higher Arboreal Instance of Appeal: this tree was not

the neighbor's own but belonged to anyone with eyes.
I told Dennis I was borrowing his word *sly*. What would

he say about *bzzz*, the sound of his death in Somerville?

51

Part II: The Dead Man Refuses To Be Used

The sawman got almost to the top, then his pulpit stopped.
He incised a wedge of space in the trunk, lassoed the crown

and gestured to his pulping friend (offstage) to pull. Again:
to make it clear that it was time. The pulper pulled, the sawman

incised in the opposite side, the crown snapped and hung
invert. No miles of writing will make new veins in pulp.

Maybe Dennis meant, *Measure absences in sky,*
two lines at a time, hold the sigh. The empty window

wonders what shape sky could take without the tree's
convexity. Then Dennis says, *You lend the blade a hand,*

you know, in making this. Were topics in short supply? And:
Tricky business, two lines at a time, making a dead man die.

I try to measure his presence in *sly.*

Cire perdue

1

You say *Nothing's missing.* I point: where there was wind, was rustle, was hush of light, was a squirrel unfurled tapping the branch down, was a lurking bird twitching on two feet. Five trees gone, and I'm still standing. So seared. So sorry you can't see behind my eyes such green demeanor as I remember, such radiant shade. What thisness they'd have brought your mind, swimming in living with all their limbs; now nothing brought, now no green thought: low plants only, and high wires. Monday Ruesday Endsday, the sun still comes up, looking for leaves to feed.

2

History is this: I was lying awake nights when you were gametes unacquainted. I rummage in fact, wonder what will suffice to fill you in, debate how truly to tell. The dead person whose name you wear wore a different smile from yours. Breathy gap between two front teeth squared and forthright, fine lines spreading in lifted lips, blooded burgundy, crosshatch brown. *And how did her mouth sound?* Like Pola Negri, ticking through projectors, slick with lipstick. Mouth slackened one day, started to stiffen, jaw got tied shut with a towel. *Then where did the kiss go?*

3

I consult in Paris with experts in absence, search a bar where John is not, see not an empty bar and not the others tippling there, but *pas-Jean.* Which fills my mind: *pas mal,* the *isn't* that persists. My mind twitches on two feet. Yet I thought to fly.

4

A man is molded by the landscape of his homeland, wrote the poet Tchernichovsky—in reinvented Hebrew, in disputed Palestine. I wish his name was pleasanter to pronounce. I wish my shape was consonant with hill and dale, leaf or branch. History has ticked forward; I still lie awake some nights. Outside of Poland, Pola will never have a speaking role. In Poland she had another name and a thisness swimming.

53

Winding Sheet

Up the stale steps
in the breathy attic,

    I confront a drawer.
    Did ever a bare ass

        rest on this maple chair?
        With what part does one

    touch life? Hands ply it
    from inside fingers;

memory's a chaste glove.
Sudden on the tongue

        by turns come *schmaltz*
        and herring. Then scraping

        of a knife on rye, then
        poppy seeds peristaltic

    in medias res. —How are you
    feeling? I ask. *—Touch wood,*

she says, *heart burn.* Small
square drawer sliding open has

    a bobbin in it. She
    is content to mind

        that bottom thread,
        loop and meet the needle

    plunging—touch wood,
    through a tiny hole

in metal, touch wood—
with circumferential logic,

    thank God, touch wood.
    Who sets the tension?

        Sewing notions hurry
        curtains, ruffle passions,

    defy scansion, touch
    life, touch wood.

        *

The seam has since been slit. I lay
the attic all to rest: stitchers and

    chewers and pickers of bits
    of herring from their teeth.

        Seeders of bread, renderers
        of chicken skin, surface into

    essence. Linkers of days
    in a line like sausage,

sitters together on the
edges of beds, sitters on

    the edges of beds in the
    altogether. Frayed ends

        of threads kick up their
        little heels, then get plucked

    from the seam now clean,
    touch wood. Touch.

III

Tortoise Shell on a Windowsill

Wellfleet, Cape Cod

The inhabitant is out, apparently
gouged. Now we can study pure
shelter. Waxy chitin, regular ridges,

brown-and-yellow fields pressing past
their boundaries on a hillside. Arching
horn inspired Song ceramics and later

eyeglass frames looking little like
this helmet for the heart and gut
that a laggard engineered to surmount

himself. Cobwebs and dust, spiders and
mites squat here. Spine inside, vestigial or
provisional, lathed into a fragile, bitten bone.

In my hand the undershell clacks against
the hill's insides, like the cover on
the plastic cup that housed my grandmother's

teeth. Some housing is intrinsic: you
secrete a home and hope for space enough
to turn in, for love to clack against your wall

so you can say, *Come in, I'll just
slide my tectonic plate aside,*
quaking. Myself, I'm renting here.

The Fragrance of Lilacs

Lilacs are nowhere to be seen

when this happens, on the flowered couch.

Nothing before, nothing

after. It happens along and above and below

and beside and with and

in. Inside within. It happens

to the two of us, versy

turvy, feet against an arm

rest. Much is against.

Much is for. How arresting! Much is laughing,

though *ha ha,* some say, is incompatible with

upheaval. When it happens lilacs

are forgotten. Nothing is

conceived, nothing is

resolved; nothing

blooming in the tapestry of havoc

is lilac. So where

does the fragrance come from and where

does it go?

How to Love

For Daniel Bosch and Lisa Lee, June 28, 2008

Allegro ma non tanto. Alleg-
retto. Allegro assai. Allegro appassionato. Andante
cantabile. Andante con moto. Sehr langsame Viertel.
Allegro amabile. Allegro

non troppo. Sehr lebhaft
markiert und kraftvoll. Allegro con brio. Allegro
vivace. Adagio. Molto adagio. Molto vivace. Allegro
con spirito. Animato. Pizzi-

cato. Poco a poco. Espres-
sivo. Etwas täppisch. Allegro animando. Etwas täppisch
und sehr derb. Allegro moderato. Sehr trotzig. Allegro
giusto. Lento e languente.

Leggieramente. Resoluto.
Allegro aperto. Allegro con fuoco. Andante. Andan-
tino. Andantino in modo di canzone. Dolce. Resoluto.
Sostenuto. Sostenuto. Sostenuto.

Safari

The Ark, Aberdare National Park, Kenya

Aground on the central highland, they speculate before first light.
  Leopard sighted to the east, says he.

She spies no feint in the grasses, no spots massing to spring.

Darkness glints from the water hole. They snap shots from a blind.

To the north, three bushbuck at the salt lick harken, start, lick, twitch,
  dart, stop.

Sky yawns pink around a flint Mt. Kenya, bares its snow teeth.

Sun gets punctured on those ridges, says he, his arm circuiting her ribs.

A gray heron steams out of rock, pure *S*-shape in air, almost not there.

Sighting! Sleepers bound out of bed, binoculars turning east together.

Maybe they'll see truly this time, through grasses, a tuft, a tussock on a
  hillock.

Gone again, says he, *may next come around the north side. May I come
  around sometime?*

News flies across breakfast tables, over spiced tea with milk, over
  marmalade on toast: the leopard jumped a bushbuck and
  mangled its throat.

Elephants in big skin stand like eons, snuffling up minerals the earth
  offers its own.

By all means, says she.

Three bushbuck at the salt lick harken, start, lick, twitch, dart, stop.

Postcard (Sky)

Hula Valley, Israel

Clots of gray herons, not clots, hordes, not
hordes, whole photogenic demographics
huddled, barking, on the ground.

Not gray, taking off, but flaxen. Not flax- but
flux-colored, air-colored, tint of dis-
appearance, hue of cry.

Snap flight and get pure sky, get *farther*, get
ever, at most the dot in *soaring*, mirrored
pupil of the famished eye.

Among the reeds a twelve-month heron dips
and staggers, trying out a courting
dance, putting on the look.

Couple for a Wedding Cake

Maasai maiden, elongated, uplifted, canted of
neck, now gentled by a Giacometti man, both
ambitious to accommodate to current trends, to

endeavor to engender long infants who might grow
toward the apex of progress. Her mock mahogany
ersatz ebony plainwood will rebound from walls of

plaster and grief. His metal, will it, under pressure,
snap, fatigued? Side by side, as yet unsynthesized, her
hands fastened to hips, his alloy arms balancing

a bold if rigid stride, no splinters in her heart
(and how would feeling help?), no oxidation at
his hingeless elbows: two taut souls attain reckless
heaven-heights as feet stick fast in frosting.

Who and Whom

The two sat together at their
dining table. I have long looked in

at lighted windows saying
Would that were I. They

spoke of *do* and *re,* tinking stainless,
pinging glass. Who said

The rim must hug the plate more
tightly. Space, please, between

the knife and spoon was said by
Whom. Folded napkins clapped

as only damask knows to do. Candles
flinched in the small wind of *so.*

Venus Paints Her Nails

(A piece for four hands)

Always careful to be no dumb
broad with artificial anything, but here
are ten small canvases on which to think
red thoughts. Broad strokes on rivers of
horn with banks to keep her inside

the lines. She covers half-moons
and sees them surface many tides later,
measures growth through slow erosion, puts
gloss down so as to get back matte. If
fingers can hold double thoughts,

Venus is less lost. Flung around
the sun, all gravity and suavity, earnestly
elliptical, with two centers, fingers forward
for the drying touch of solar wind. She
presto from celestial ivories coaxes

silence in a minor key turning
to open something, dips into shine
of stars long dead for a final protective
coat, playing—smudgelessly—
every accidental with intent.

Slut

I will go wherever a few lines might
come together. Gentlemen, you

don't want to know this about me
but it is the *almost* and the *after* I

am after, the chosen pickins,
the gate in no fence around

a pasture, the peckish apéritif,
the weed between the tree, and oh, you

too, if I can bear you, heft my
half, parse the *must* in *us*.

But I prefer the angled glance
off the edge of an eyeful,

suggestive weather by dint of
round mint on the pillow, not

the full weight of a truffle
on the tongue, well maybe

full clench of tenses
present and passing

long enough for me to take
notes and you to pay the bill.

IV

Turner I

Painting Parliament burning, Turner reverses
the drift of the wind so the river can echo yellow

with red reverberations as crowds on boats observe
the melding of towers and time, and all parties puddle

in conflations of paint. Bad buildings deserve,
some hold, to ashen in their heap. Now as cinders

descend, leaders will be better. Reform will infuse
the air, new laws sprout out of stone as soon as

the paint dries. But rivulets of thinner subvert,
and winds once unleashed in a lie rarely return.

Turner II

Life I find don't you is full of interruption. The clothes out of a dryer and where to fold them and how long do they hold their warmth. For *The Burning of the Houses of Parliament* Turner reversed the direction of the wind so that flames went toward the Thames, maximizing reflection. In life I like to maximize reflection don't you. If you fold them on the basement table you have to carry piles upstairs like a cartoon chef with a flapjack stack. *Where's the insurance* the woman was saying *I'm no spring chicken, what if the house burns down*. He said *bouillon bouillon bouillon* in the French way. In life I like to go up stairs with *crêpes* don't you. If you bring them up to fold them on the bed will you drop socks. Nanny said *mais non non non Eloise* and best in the book was the uncombable hair. Life I find is largely uncombable don't you. That warm towels would be so reassuring in this day and age when attacks in the desert follow fighting between north and south so I've stopped reading the news. The gas dryer is controlled wind and fire so who can blame Turner for his lie. I see in my diary from last October that Botticelli gave up beauty for Savonarola and I want to make something of it don't you. If you bring them up not to lie but to maximize reflection. Those refugee camps like stage sets with smoke rising, those *Times* photographers I'll bet lugging dry ice. If you are a lonely child or a child of any onlyness you want to be somewhere close-knit like say the Plaza. Willy-nilly there are people around but willy-nilly is a thing of the past. Now we have intention don't you. If your name was Turner would you paint straight. Some surfboard sails have a clear vinyl window through which you see the wind, your motor and motive, looking back. Life I find looking back is full of motor and motive don't you. Was Botticelli's conversion caused by Turner's inversion. His revulsion at rivulets of thinner, paint forever wet. What if you rode in the dryer, unfolding all winter. Or were paint in an open can swung round and round and *non non non Eloise:* suddenly centripetal, you spatter all over gravity. Fun is not the word. But wait a minute I'll tell you what is.

Meditation: Anything Can Come Here

1

I open my eyes to the lake and sit
unnoticed. The barking dog found

other, better bones. Lapping water
addresses the rock. The frog leaps

clear of my mind, where I ascend
invented steps as I lay them down.

Grasses waving their arms in the lake
require no rescue. The wind on my face

stirs the dust on the steps. I give no one
directions; I am as lost as found.

2

This is not a suture, but the puncture
where a thread might run. Surgeon,

spider, seamster are on leave.
The span of silence is immenser than

the watershed of blood in veins. I say
not *never*, just *not*. Perhaps *perhaps*.

3

In an armchair at the town café,
a girl in elegant sandals dozes,

an open book resting on her chest:
La guerra infinita: Hegemonia y

terror mundial. Chestnut tresses lap at
the glossy cover. The book rises and falls.

4

A perfect composition of clouds
unravels. My eyes relinquish

green bristle of trees across the lake.
On the forest floor, bands of

white-birch bark embrace their
splinters; my own crumbling cortex

relaxes its grasp. Some cut timber has
ripples like water. I need not invent

the stone that dropped there.
Anything can come here

and sit down in its description, then
amble at will into white space.

5

I tell the mosquito: I am elsewhere.
The mosquito brings a friend.

To the Bomber of the Holy City Hardware

I went in for a drill
and came out
on both sides of my skin.

I know your terror.
Once I killed a cat
and put my hands inside
to feel the last lapping.

Here's me, welling
and ebbing like sun on
the sea over slivers
of glass.

Neighbor, I'm listening now.

Farming in the Jezreel Valley

Get the cotton in
before the first rain, reap the
first rain before the pond's face
drops, dig the pond a place before the
mountain's built, get the mountain grown
before the city sits on it and stops its breath.
To say nothing of guns.

The Hebrew name
of the former rain
is the same as *shoot*,
and it goes through you
like the sharpest season.
The latter rain:
malkosh, a splash
of craters in dry dirt.

Skittish summer dreams
more hills into the landscape
till the farmer's out of wits.
What he plants in the cabbage patch
comes up in the cotton as
Earth wobbles out from under.
Only the olive sinks its
own spot, sticks to living
till the meaty purple burst.
Most get eaten first.

They Run

They run. In every generation some run on every continent,
mostly Africa, often Asia, used to be Europe, never Antarctica
though penguins hurry. Even America north of
the Great Equator. They run. Sometimes the continent drifts and
they cannot but shift back with equal and opposite
perturbation. I'm saying this more slowly than it happens.
They run in only two syllables, right left right left, those that
have both options still. They run in dust, grit coating
the insides of their open mouths. They used to run with
baskets and satchels and duffels, now
backpacks and laptops and iPods. Some
hang back to pack, some just go sans portmanteau. Some sew
into the lining of whatever cloak remains things
fathers bestowed before they ran, but
these days what fabric has backing? Some, running in summer, notice
green sun glowing through luminous leaves at 4 a.m., but find in
dawning beauty a betrayal. Always it is too late, always
is *all ways* where time equals distance and everyone
runs. Some run shouting *Where is*, shouting *Grab him
leave her* then equal and opposite *Grab her leave
him*, those that have both options still. They run. Some tie
the doll to the child's wrist, circle the child with a fence in the
mind, padlock the mind, bury the key by the planted tree,
then run. Someone pushes Nana in a handcart to the border,
where guards barter, then balk. They run. Nana
can be Granny, sometimes Mima Oma Savta. Always a trochee
with an open end, a feminine rhyme, like the skin that
smiles on the bottoms of her feet, then laughs itself
away. She runs. Coming round a corner, men for days unshaven

glimpse themselves in windows and scare at the sight. They run.
They run through wheat fields and rice paddies, yank
a gourd off the ground, but also through trolley barns, strip malls,
        empty
market stalls where turnips roll off a table. *Grab them Leave*
them say those that have both options still. They run. There remains
in the middle of the road a sandal slapping air with its arc of
strap. They run. Some in torrents run like salmon
against the waters for their lives and for their
spawn. Mud sucks their boots off. They run. Inside-out around
them buildings are turning, people too outwearing their
innards in cries. Listen to the rustle of
the lining. When it comes our time to run all
ways may we, on a late green day, betray.

Proclamation

Following the cease-fire at 0700
rivers will flow from east to west.
          Blue is mauve as of midnight. Crags
          are henceforth peaks; goats are barred
from paths that serve mountain lions;
turds will be pats. True, there were
          expulsions but they were voluntary
          and deserved. Lives ended because
they were wrong. Women and children,
being weaker, ended sooner. That young
          boys stand stupidly in the line of fire is
          neither blue nor mauve but universal.
Universe and *mauve* have in common
the victory *V*. Letters addressed in blue
          will be read under streetlights recently
          extinguished. Extinction to be weighed
also for certain cerulean skies. Honor to
ancestors! Our *begat*s have long been
          poaching in parchment; this is the first
          of many tastings. Mauve bones inhabit
our native hills and fragrance our native
air. Restrict your breezes to the far side
          of hedges and toss your passports HERE.
          You failed to straighten your streams.
Your people are nomads and shiftless;
squinting cosmopolites. All whistling
          will issue henceforth from mauve
          lips. The water in your former lakes
is ours. We have stenciled superior names
over your street signs, planted our flags in
          your former gardens. You are free to
          watch them grow.

Possible Poem: Rivers on Which
I Have Seen Light Dance

It would be a list, would link geography of source
and salt. The tongue would taste varietal place in

mere pronouncement. The possible poem would
leave out cars behind me noising through puddles

on New Year's, would ask tall buildings across
the river to break their silence, would maybe put

words in their mouths. But why devise brick-speak,
statements of glaze? White tarps on boats inflate

in wind, disguising edges. Must poems be of
honest lineation? The year began dryly, a distant

friend rustling meager greeting like the crinkly
bag at my feet, plastic in wind. I stare down

skyscrapers glinting across currents. Conceits row
slowly, puddles muddy. How the tsunami hungered

for the mud of human making. Here a weathervane
jitters in sun. I can't see what moves it, though

I feel its pointlessness. A boy strides by
in search of a better answer. On some days

poems are not possible. So as sun lights
indifferently on the page, I eat an apple.

Please taste *eat* as carefully as you can.

To My Translator

Maybe the lunge to the sideward, your
lip ballet, equals the hardest case, squatty

with concision, straightway askance. The reasons
for this are numerable. All the appurtenances, I am

accessible to say, mark their leave somewhere.
This is the only one of mandates I come to you

bearing: hand me into this new space, think with me
the multiplication of tables, the last of shoes.

How particulate the writhing trees, where
my heart is windy: are you hearing its air?

One can transfer parts of our self throughout
these lines. Please to be the who to transverse.

Rapture

Having watched
   icy spare stars into
      the night I wake
tired but other.

Sun is brash, trees
   are mere near
      sticks, towering. Green
is eye ache, excessive,

bluebells and all other
   chiming blooms a tinny
      afterthought painted
into the real world in

a studio on the Arno.
   I can't wait to
      get back to night glitter,
X-ray of evermore,

expanding. Stars go so
   much deeper into
      darkness than these
anthills and vole

holes in the daily
   upslope. I say to
      the lights *Come get*
me I'm ready. Then an

upsurge of
   indirection: cloud cover.
      Just tell me which
way to turn my

face, where to put my
    mere near sticks of
        bone, flowering, how
to brush off loam.

Corner

Not just the car turning the corner while all the trees stand still,
not just deceleration, gears grinding as birds assess degrees of leaf
with silver intervals in green interrogation, not just downshift
and the red gems of blinkers and the looking-all-ways that the
driver does, and the treads of tires picking up pebbles skidding
across asphalt, not just the car turning the corner as geraniums
turn their heat up high, pebbles uprising across geranium blaze
under coughs of exhaust of acceleration as the angle of the new
street opens wide to the car turning the corner and wind dogs
buoyant branches, braiding itself through a Cyclone fence past
serried city house fronts: rather, more broadly, what moves and
what waits. And this too is a day of grace, provided we keep our
tires inflated to the pressure recommended in the manual and
the gas pump is up to its neck in octane and our enemies have
not yet ignited the pipeline and the tanker has not leaked its
innards into the bay while the dockers slide their lunches out of
brown bags, flap open butcher paper, widen their mouths
around the sliced cheeses called American and the sliced meats
called cold cuts even in this heat: dockers with pebbles in the
treads of their palms dotting and dashing the line called heart
and the line called head and the line called fate: what moves and
what awaits, as the corner is turned by the car.

The *Illustrated* Edge

Sometimes an edge is a corner, in which case you do not fall off. Corners are achieved by urging one plane into another, then feeling slatted and fenced (fig. 1). The planes feel otherwise, each at its own tilt.

Sometimes an edge is a border, in which case you see more of the same, maybe rippling grass, but hear it calling to itself in another tongue. You can put your toe over. It may turn a different color, like from *bala'ti* to *palavrata*, or from pencil to ink. Music switches scales (fig. 2). Fish swim dorsal-down in that other hemisphere. Sometimes, given atmospheric change and mines, your toe explodes. Caution is advised. Pedicures are available. Nothing is forever cured by crossing fine lines.

Sometimes an edge takes to a table, in which case there are drips and crumbs and bellies pressed up close. Digestion is heard, also hunger (fig. 3), sometimes bookish crinkly thoughts, usually black on a cream ground, a smoothness pressed into texture. Elbows attend, indecisive, poise-or-plunge.

Sometimes an edge is rounded, as in the egg, in which case things fall off, such as the bloom first and foremost. The rounded edge is in dispute between the plane and arc, hence Archimedes' mediation these two thousand years, and Earth so far unmoved. This edge is incremental in its geometry, hazardous in sin (fig. 4), endlessly holding out the hope of a center.

Notes

Table of Equivalents: Sources include Andrew Marvell's "The Garden" and "Upon Appleton House"; Joachim-Ernst Berendt, *The Third Ear: On Listening to the World*, trans. Tim Nevill (New York: Henry Holt and Company, 1992), pp. 89 and 91; Deuteronomy; and Gay Robins and Charles Shute, *The Rhind Mathematical Papyrus: An Ancient Egyptian Text* (London: British Museum Press, 1989), pp. 15 and 51, reproduced by permission of The Trustees of the British Museum. I can't remember where I found the recipe substitutions, so apply with caution.

Cow in a Gallery: The speaker is one of the two cows sliced, immersed, and interspersed in Damien Hirst's installation *Some Comfort Gained from the Acceptance of the Inherent Lies in Everything*, Gagosian Gallery, New York, 1996.

Roy G. Biv Appears to Me between Two Clouds: The name is a schoolbook mnemonic for the colors of the rainbow: red, orange, yellow, green, blue, indigo, violet.

Blind Clarissa Field and Her Doll: A doll named Bangwell Putt, born in 1770 and believed to be the oldest rag doll in America, was the lifelong companion of Clarissa Field of Northfield, Massachusetts, who couldn't see her. Bangwell is displayed on shirt cardboard in the nearby Deerfield Museum.

Acknowledgments

My thanks to the editors of the following periodicals, where these poems or earlier versions of them appeared:

Beloit Poetry Journal: "What the Tenor Does with His Hands," "*Cire perdue*," "Who and Whom"

Boston Review: "Tri-Town Paving Does a Country Road to the Strains of Bach's B-Minor Mass," "Roy G. Biv Appears to Me between Two Clouds," "Winding Sheet," "To My Translator"

Helikon: "Farming in the Jezreel Valley" in Hebrew translation

Jerusalem Post Magazine: "Farming in the Jezreel Valley"

Parnassus: Poetry in Review: "Acacia," "What Birds Mean When They Say That," "Tree"

PN Review: "Inscriptions for Chinese Paintings," "mm/dd\yy," "Safari," "Possible Poem: Rivers on Which I Have Seen Light Dance"

Puckerbrush Review: "The *Illustrated* Edge"

Salamander: "Slut," "Corner"

Stand: "To the Bomber of the Holy City Hardware"

Two If By Sea (newsletter, MIT/Woods Hole Oceanographic Institution Sea Grant Programs): "Tortoise Shell on a Windowsill"

The MacDowell Colony and the Massachusetts Cultural Council gave me recognition and support at crucial times.

For attentive reading, time, space, gentle lucre, kind words, and/or company along the way, I alphabetize and gratefully acknowledge: Daniel Bosch, Andrea Cohen, Kinereth Gensler, Neil Hertz, Edwin Honig, Becky Hunt, Lisa Lee, Herb Leibowitz, Liz Levey, Gabriel Levin, Bill Marx, Eric Ormsby, Dorothy and Zvi Pantanowitz, Bob and Ellen Pomerantz, Dennis Priebe, Miriam and Joe Slipowitz, Dan Wells, and Susan Yankowitz.

About the Author

Marsha Pomerantz grew up in New York, lived in Israel for twenty years, and now lives in Boston. Her poems and prose have been published in journals in the US, UK, and Israel, and she has translated poetry, short fiction, and a novel from the Hebrew. Her writing has been supported by two residencies at the MacDowell Colony and by a Massachusetts Cultural Council finalist grant, and she has twice been a finalist for the Poetry Society of America's Robert H. Winner Award. She is managing editor at the Harvard Art Museums.